BEHIND THE CURTAIN
Act Out History's BIGGEST Dramas

ESCAPE NORTH

UNDERGROUND RAILROAD

Virginia Loh-Hagan

45th Parallel Press

Published in the United States of America by Cherry Lake Publishing
Ann Arbor, Michigan
www.cherrylakepublishing.com

Reading Adviser: Marla Conn MS, Ed., Literacy specialist, Read-Ability, Inc.
Book Designer: Felicia Macheske

Photo Credits: © Jacob_09/Shutterstock.com, cover, 1; Highsmith (Carol M.) Archive, Library of Congress, LC-DIG-highsm-32050, 5; Library of Congress, LC-DIG-ppmsca-54375, 6; Library of Congress, LC-DIG-det-4a27014, 11; Library of Congress, LC-DIG-ppmsca-15836, 12; © Everett Historical/Shutterstock.com, 17, 21, 25; Library of Congress, LC-DIG-ppmsca-54230, 18; © EvgeniiAnd/Shutterstock.com, 23; © Instants/iStock.com, 29

Graphic Elements Throughout: © Chipmunk131/Shutterstock.com; © Nowik Sylwia/Shutterstock.com; © Andrey_Popov/Shutterstock.com; © NadzeyaShanchuk/Shutterstock.com; © KathyGold/Shutterstock.com; © Black creator/Shutterstock.com; © Edvard Molnar/Shutterstock.com; © Elenadesign/Shutterstock.com; estherpoon/Shutterstock.com

45th Parallel Press is an imprint of Cherry Lake Publishing.

Library of Congress Cataloging-in-Publication Data has been filed and is available at catalog.loc.gov

Cherry Lake Publishing would like to acknowledge the work of The Partnership for 21st Century Skills. Please visit www.p21.org for more information.

Printed in the United States of America
Corporate Graphics

A Note on Dramatic Retellings

Participating in Readers Theater, or dramatic retellings, can greatly improve reading skills, especially fluency. The books in the **BEHIND THE CURTAIN** series give readers opportunities to learn about important historical events in a fun and engaging way. These books serve as a bridge to more complex texts. All the characters are real figures from history; however, their stories have been fictionalized. To learn more about the people and the events, check out the Viewpoints and Perspectives series and the Perspectives Library series, as the **BEHIND THE CURTAIN** books are aligned to these stories.

TABLE of CONTENTS

HISTORICAL BACKGROUND

Slaves were being bought and sold in the United States. The government was letting it happen. People were taken from Africa. They were forced to work on **plantations** in the South. Many people thought this was wrong. **Abolitionists** were against slavery. They wanted to free the slaves.

Slaves escaped. They ran away from the **slave states** in the South. They ran to the **free states** in the North. They ran to Canada. Some ran to Mexico.

The Underground Railroad helped **fugitive** slaves. It was a secret **system**. It had **safe houses**. It had hiding places. It had secret roads. It was formed in the late 1700s. It was most popular around the 1850s.

FLASH FACT!

During the Civil War, the Mason-Dixon line was the border between Southern and Northern states.

Vocabulary

slaves (SLAYVZ) people who are stolen from their homes and forced to do work

plantations (plan-TAY-shuhnz) big farms

abolitionists (ab-uh-LISH-uh-nists) people who fought against slavery

slave states (SLAYV STAYTS) states that allowed slavery

free states (FREE STAYTS) states that did not allow slavery

fugitive (FYOO-jih-tiv) runaway

system (SIS-tuhm) organizational plan

safe houses (SAYF HOUS-iz) houses that provide protection

FLASH FACT!

Fugitive slaves faced many hardships.

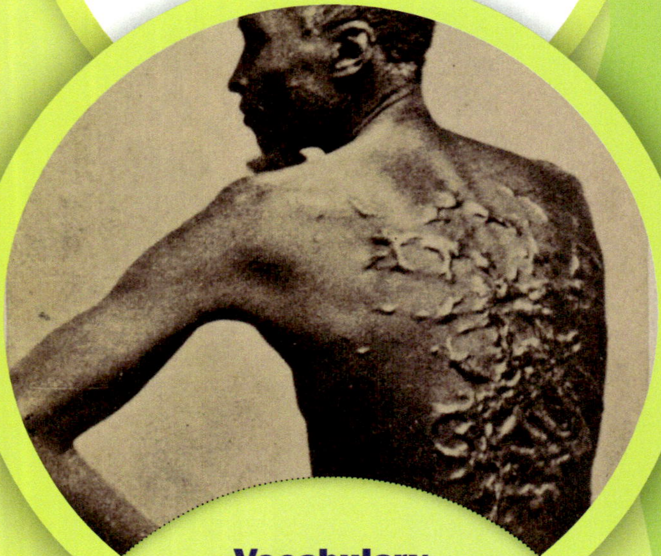

Vocabulary

codes (KOHDZ) messages in a secret language

conductors (kuhn-DUHKT-urz) people who act as guides

agents (AY-juhnts) people who help others

stations (STAY-shuhnz) buildings where passengers come and go

passengers (PAS-uhn-jurz) people who travel

People passed notes to the slaves. They sent secret **codes**. They did this in songs. They did this by marking trees. They helped guide slaves from place to place. They were called **conductors**. Some people were "**agents**." They made clothes. They collected money. They taught slaves to read and write. The safe houses were called **stations**. Slaves were called **passengers**.

The Underground Railroad was dangerous business. Helping slaves was against the law. When caught, people were punished. It was especially risky for fugitive slaves. Slaves could get killed. For many, freedom was worth it. The Underground Railroad saved over 100,000 slaves.

CAST of CHARACTERS

NARRATOR: person who helps tell the story

MAJOR BENJAMIN CHAIRES: owner of Verdura Plantation in Florida that makes cotton, slave owner

THOMAS FULTON: slave owner, **tobacco** farmer in Tennessee

JOSIAH BRAXTON: 17-year-old fugitive slave from Kentucky who escapes to Ohio

HENRY BIBB: fugitive slave who escapes to Canada

HARRIET TUBMAN: former slave who escaped from Maryland to Pennsylvania, most famous conductor who is sometimes called **Moses**

EMMA JACKSON: housewife living in Maryland, conductor who hides slaves in her home

BACKSTORY
SPOTLIGHT BIOGRAPHY

Some Native Americans helped slaves. They fought in slave rebellions. They hid slaves. They helped guide them to the North. Their trails were a path to freedom. In some cases, Native Americans and slaves got married. They had children. Diana Fletcher was an example. Not much is known about her. But it's believed that she was a "Black Indian." Her father was a slave. He ran away. He lived with a Native American tribe. He married a Seminole woman. Her mother died in the Trail of Tears. This is when the government moved Native Americans off their lands. Fletcher was born in 1838. She was separated from her parents. She was adopted by a Kiowa family. She learned how to do Kiowa arts and crafts. She taught in schools for Native American children. She tried to keep her culture. She also tried to adapt to white American culture.

Vocabulary

tobacco (tuh-BAK-oh) a plant that is used for smoking or chewing

Moses (MOH-zez) a person in the Bible who led slaves to freedom

FLASH FACT!

Many Quakers, including Levi Coffin, gave shelter to slaves.

ACT 1

NARRATOR: *It's the late 1850s.* **THOMAS FULTON** *and* **MAJOR BENJAMIN CHAIRES** *are in town. They're buying farm* **supplies***. They're talking in a shop. They're in a Southern slave state.*

BENJAMIN: How's your farm doing?

THOMAS: This year has been great. I'm selling a lot of tobacco. How about you?

BENJAMIN: Everyone seems to want cotton. My cotton is sent to Northern states. It's even sent to Great Britain. I had to buy more slaves.

THOMAS: Buying slaves is cheaper than paying workers. That's the only way I can make money. My farm would **go under** without **slave labor**.

BENJAMIN: Those abolitionists are such pests. They're calling for the end of slavery. The Northern states don't get it. They want our products. But they don't like how we do things.

Vocabulary

supplies (suh-PLYEZ) equipment needed for a purpose

go under (GOH UHN-dur) go out of business

slave labor (SLAYV LAY-bur) work done by slaves

FLASH FACT!

Before the Civil War, cotton made in the South was 77 percent of the cotton processed in British mills.

THOMAS: The slave system is what makes the U.S. rich. The South would break without it. Those abolitionists need to stop **complaining**.

BENJAMIN: I heard slaves are running away. Are you worried about that?

THOMAS: None of my slaves have run away. They have no reason to run. I treat them well. Plus, it's too dangerous. Slaves don't have any **resources**. They don't own winter clothes or shoes. Only a few can read or write. And none of them have seen a map.

BENJAMIN: They also get badly punished. Some of those slave catchers are **brutal**.

NARRATOR: *It's late at night.* **JOSIAH BRAXTON** *and* **HENRY BIBB** *are deep in the woods.*

JOSIAH: Look for the North Star.

HENRY: We're supposed to wait for the conductor.

Vocabulary

complaining (kuhm-PLAYN-ing) whining or grumbling

resources (REE-sors-iz) money, supplies, etc.

brutal (BROO-tuhl) harsh, cruel, mean

FLASH FACT!

Between 1790 and 1808, nearly 80,000 slaves were brought to the United States to work cotton.

JOSIAH: I heard Moses herself will be meeting us.

HENRY: Harriet Tubman is so brave. She's saved over 300 slaves.

JOSIAH: Slavery is wrong. How can one man own another man?

HENRY: Why did you run?

JOSIAH: The master died. His wife and son were going to sell me. They were going to send me farther south. I **refuse** to be sold like a horse. One of the slave girls sang a song. I knew it was code. I had to take my chance. What about you?

HENRY: The master rented me out to others. He needed money to pay for his daughter's schooling. I did all kinds of work. But the master was never happy. He was always whipping me. Then, he caught me learning to read.

LOCATION SHOOTING

REAL-WORLD SETTING

The Ohio River runs from Pittsburgh, Pennsylvania, to Cairo, Illinois. It's 981 miles (1,579 kilometers) long. It flows along the borders of six states. It marked the border between slave and free states. It was known as the River Jordan. In the Bible, people crossed the Jordan River to freedom. The Ohio River played a big part in the Underground Railroad. Many slaves crossed this river to freedom. When slaves were caught, they were sent down the Ohio River. They were sent back to the South. This meant they were "sold down the river." This is a popular saying. It means someone has been betrayed. The "Freedom Stairway" has 100 steps. It leads from the Ohio River to John Rankin's house. Rankin's house had several secret rooms. He hid runaway slaves. He put a light in the window. This meant the house was safe.

Vocabulary

refuse (rih-FYOOZ) to show that one is not willing to do something

FLASH FACT!

Overseers whipped slaves for not working hard enough.

JOSIAH: Oh no! Slaves aren't allowed to read or write. We're punished for that.

HENRY: I got beat that day. I had to run. The hard part is leaving my wife and daughter. One day, I'll return for them.

NARRATOR: **HARRIET TUBMAN** *guides* **JOSIAH BRAXTON** *and* **HENRY BIBB**. *They follow the North Star.*

HARRIET: Are you sure you want to do this? The Underground Railroad is dangerous. Everyone involved takes great risks. You could be killed.

HENRY: Slavery is already killing me. I want my freedom.

JOSIAH: It's too late to turn back now.

HARRIET: You need to promise me something. You can't tell anyone about the Underground Railroad. The masters will **torture** you. They want information. They'll do whatever they can to stop us. You must not say a word.

Vocabulary

torture (TOR-chur) to give pain as punishment

FLASH FACT!

The living conditions for slaves were bad. They were given little food and clothing.

HENRY: The Underground Railroad has **rescued** so many people. I wouldn't dare put it at risk.

JOSIAH: Same here. All we have is hope. I'd never take that away from other slaves.

HARRIET: You'll be free or die a slave!

JOSIAH: What do we need to do?

HARRIET: You can only move at night. You have to hide during the day.

HENRY: We're going to get cold. We're going to get hungry. What do we do about that?

HARRIET: There are many helpers on the Underground Railroad. People will help when they can. I'm not going to lie. There will be tough times. Don't ever stop. Keep going. If you want a taste of freedom, keep going.

Vocabulary

rescued (RES-kyood) saved

FLASH FACT!

Harriet Tubman was an inspiration to many people.

ACT 2

NARRATOR: *It's several months later.* **THOMAS FULTON** *and* **MAJOR BENJAMIN CHAIRES** *are at the police station.*

THOMAS: I'm here to report runaway slaves to the **sheriff**.

BENJAMIN: Me too.

THOMAS: My slaves found out I was selling some of them. A couple of slaves ran.

BENJAMIN: I hate the Underground Railroad. Some of my slaves have escaped as well. We need to find out who's helping them. These people are stealing my **property**. They should be punished.

THOMAS: The Fugitive Slave Act is on our side. Getting our slaves back is the law. Anyone who helps slaves will be punished. They'll have to pay **fines**. They might even be jailed. Runaway slaves will also be punished. They'll be whipped.

BENJAMIN: It's just business. We deserve to get our property back.

Vocabulary

sheriff (SHER-if) the person in charge of enforcing the law in a county or town

property (PRAH-pur-tee) things owned by a person

fines (FINEZ) fees

FLASH FACT!

Even if fugitives made it to free states, they could be taken back to the South.

THOMAS: Those slaves will come back in chains. Or they'll come back dead. I'm going to hire **slave catchers**. I'm going to give a **reward**.

BENJAMIN: I've heard some slave catchers use **packs** of dogs. They hunt down slaves like animals.

THOMAS: I will get my slaves back. And the Underground Railroad people will pay for this. Life will be even harder for my slaves. No more extra food on Saturdays. No more free Sunday afternoons.

NARRATOR: **JOSIAH BRAXTON** *and* **HENRY BIBB** *have been traveling on the Underground Railroad. They're in bad shape.* **EMMA JACKSON** *has been waiting for them.*

JOSIAH: Harriet told us to look for a light in the window. She said that would be a safe house.

HENRY: I see the light. Let's go!

EMMA: Come in! Hurry! Did anyone see you?

Vocabulary

slave catchers (SLAYV KACH-urz) professionals whose job was to catch runaway slaves

reward (rih-WORD) a money prize

packs (PAKS) groups

FLASH FACT!

In 1849, there was a 300-dollar reward out for the return of Harriet Tubman and her two brothers.

JOSIAH: No one saw us. We lost the dogs at the river.

EMMA: I can't believe they're treating people in such a way. It's not right.

HENRY: Where are we?

EMMA: You're in a free state.

JOSIAH: We're free! We're finally free!

HENRY: Not really. No man is free in a country where slavery is **legal** anywhere.

Vocabulary
legal (LEE-guhl) lawful

FLASH FACT!
Fugitives traveled long distances until they found shelter.

EMMA: Henry is right. Slave catchers are everywhere. If they catch you, they'll send you back. Rest. Warm up. Eat. You need to get strong. You'll need to fight for your freedom every day.

JOSIAH: Where is your husband?

EMMA: He's getting more fugitives. He pretends to be a slave trader. Then, he leads slaves to our house. We have many secret rooms.

HENRY: Why do you help us? Aren't you afraid?

EMMA: I'm scared all the time. The laws are getting **stricter**. We could lose everything if we get caught. But slavery is wrong. No law can make me stop. I'm willing to break laws that I don't believe in.

NARRATOR: *It's many months later.* **HARRIET TUBMAN** *is at* **EMMA JACKSON'S** *house.*

EMMA: Whatever happened to Josiah?

HARRIET: He made it. He's in Ohio. He changed his name. He hasn't been caught yet.

EMMA: And what about Henry?

HARRIET: Oh, Henry! He went back for his family. He was **captured**. He was sent back to the master. His daughter got sick. She died. Henry and his wife tried to escape. They got caught. Henry's wife was sold to another man.

BLOOPERS

HISTORICAL MISTAKES

Slave owners didn't like the Underground Railroad. They were losing their slaves. So, they hunted their slaves. They pushed for the Fugitive Slave Act. This law promoted the capture of escaping slaves. It also punished people for helping slaves. This law was abused. Slave catchers weren't good people. They hurt slaves. They would take free blacks in the North. They sent them to the South. An example was Solomon Northup. He was born free. He was stolen from Washington, D.C. He was taken to Louisiana. He spent 12 years as a slave. People of color didn't have any rights. They couldn't defend themselves. They couldn't go to court. Slave catchers were white. They promised the people they caught were actually slaves. The courts had to believe them. This practice was unfair. The Fugitive Slave Act was meant to stop runaway slaves. But it just made abolitionists madder. It hurried the coming of the Civil War.

Vocabulary

stricter (STRIKT-ur) more severe

captured (KAP-churd) taken, stolen, caught

FLASH FACT!

Many slaves were separated from their families.

EMMA: Oh, my! Poor Henry.

HARRIET: There is a happy ending. Henry made a **final** escape. He's now in Canada. He's a free man.

EMMA: That's good news.

HARRIET: There's more. Henry also learned to read and write. He started a newspaper. He shares his story. He's an abolitionist now.

EMMA: Josiah and Henry are the **success** stories. But there are so many sad stories. So many people have died. So many people didn't make it.

HARRIET: If we helped one person, it was worth it. An **enslaved** person lives an **inhumane** life. My goal is to help free all those who suffer as I have.

EMMA: I wish more folks would join us.

HARRIET: This work is not for everyone. It's dangerous. But it's important. Helpers are everywhere. We're not alone.

Vocabulary

final (FYE-nuhl) last time

success (suhk-SES) the accomplishment of a goal

enslaved (en-SLAYVD) made someone a slave

inhumane (in-HYOO-mayn) not human, not kind

FLASH FACT!

Henry Bibb was recaptured several times.

EVENT TIMELINE

- **1619:** The first African slaves are brought into Great Britain's North American colonies. They're taken to Jamestown, Virginia.
- **1794:** Eli Whitney invents the cotton gin. This causes a huge demand for slave labor.
- **1790s:** Isaac Hopper begins organizing a network of safe spaces. He starts the Underground Railroad.
- **1820:** The first long-distance route of the Underground Railroad is set up. Fugitive slaves travel from North Carolina to Indiana.
- **1826:** Quakers in Indiana help slaves. They build secret rooms in their homes. They build fake bottoms in their wagons.
- **1830:** David Ruggles and Isaac Hopper build a network in New York City. This helps over 6,000 slaves.
- **1841:** Josiah Henson starts a school for former slaves. He does this in Canada. He teaches skills. He provides job training.
- **1849:** Harriet Tubman escapes from slavery. She runs from Maryland to Pennsylvania. She returns to Maryland many times. She helps slaves escape.
- **March 29, 1849:** Henry Box Brown escapes slavery. He gets into a box. He mails himself from Virginia to Pennsylvania.
- **September 18, 1850:** The Fugitive Slave Act is passed. The United States bans efforts to stop the capture of runaway slaves. Abolitionists protest. They support the Underground Railroad.
- **March 6, 1857:** The Dred Scott decision is passed. African Americans can't be citizens.
- **November 6, 1860:** Abraham Lincoln is elected the U.S. president.
- **1861–1865:** The Civil War takes place. Northern and Southern states fight against each other. The main issue is slavery.
- **January 1, 1863:** President Lincoln signs the Emancipation Proclamation. This frees all slaves in the Southern states.
- **December 18, 1865:** The 13th Amendment to the U.S. Constitution passes. It bans slavery.

CONSIDER THIS!

TAKE A POSITION! The Underground Railroad was a path to freedom. But it was also dangerous. Was freedom worth the dangers? Harriet Tubman said, "There are two things I had a right to: liberty cr death. If I could not have one, I would have the other, for no man should take me alive." What does this mean? Do you agree or disagree? Argue your point with reasons and evidence.

SAY WHAT? Learn more about Harriet Tubman. Explain how she's connected to the Underground Railroad. Explain why she's important. Explain why she's called Moses.

THINK ABOUT IT! What are the risks of being a conductor? Would you have helped slaves escape? Why or why not? Would you have been brave enough? Not everyone in this world is being treated fairly. Identify one group. Learn about the issues. What can you do to help?

LEARN MORE

Cummings, Judy Dodge, and Tom Casteel (illust.). *The Underground Railroad: Navigate the Journey from Slavery to Freedom with 20 Projects*. White River Junction, VT: Nomad Press, 2017.

Llanas, Sheila Griffin. *The Underground Railroad*. Ann Arbor, MI: Cherry Lake Publishing, 2014.

McDonough, Yona Zeldis. *What Was the Underground Railroad?* New York: Grosset & Dunlap, 2013.

Russo, Kristin J. *Viewpoints on the Underground Railroad*. Ann Arbor, MI: Cherry Lake Publishing, 2019.

INDEX

ABOUT THE AUTHOR

Dr. Virginia Loh-Hagan is an author, university professor, and former classroom teacher. She works on being "woke." She hopes everyone else is doing the same. She lives in San Diego with her very tall husband and very naughty dogs.